Breaking Army and Air Force Enigma

Edited by John Jackson

Contents

Introduction	2
General	3
Reflector D The first menace; The BO mystery; Greenshank and D; D-Breaks; Summary of the German use of D	4
Zusatz Stecker A damp squib; Extent of change	7
Enigma Uhr The problem; Extension of Uhr; Uhr notation; Summary	8
NOT-Schlüssel Introduction; First system; Guernsey saga and the Forty NOTS; New-style NOT-keys; Conclusions	10
C Y Introduction; Effect on breaking; Conclusion	14
Random Indicators Introduction; Conclusion	14
Wahlworts Introduction; Extension of wahlworts; Use of wahlworts; Effect on breaking; Value of wahlworts	15
The Mosse Code	18
Double encoding	19
Summary and Conclusions General; How breaks were secured; How breaks could have been prevented; The two roads; The principle of over-protection	20
The German Enigma The failure of German efforts; Air and Army security; The special case of Greenshank; How to achieve security	22
The necessity of supervision	24

Introduction

Bletchley Park's (BP) battle to break into the secret messages of the German armed forces and security services in World War II was a never-ending struggle. The Germans were not static, but were dreaming up new ways to make the "unbreakable" Enigma cipher machine even more secure. This constant struggle is underlined in the three volumes of the Bletchley Park End-of-War Report *The History of Hut 6,* which can be found in the National Archives under HW 43/72.

This deals with the breaking of German Army and Air ciphers as well as Police, SS, the railways and the V-weapons.

The contents of this booklet do not deal with the battle to break German naval Enigma messages, in itself an epic struggle, nor does it attempt to make a comprehensive study of the entire area of breaking Enigma messages, the subject of which, from the Hut 6 Official History, took three volumes!

It examines, in the words of those who wrote these end-of-war reports – although edited for brevity – nine particular security devices which put BP's Hut 6 on its mettle. These were:

Reflector D
The pluggable reflector introduced in January 1944 on the German Air Force cipher "Red", and later on other GAF keys and some Army keys.

Enigma Uhr
An attachment to the Enigma machine, whereby the stecker (plugboard) of individual messages on the same key could be varied.

Zusatz Stecker
A security device, whereby two of the stecker pairings were altered during the course of the day.

NOT-Schlüssel
An emergency key, especially constructed from a given Schlüsselwort – a word from which the NOT-key was derived.

C Y
A security device, by which the position of the left-hand wheel was altered during the encoding of a message, the new position being indicated to the decoder by the letters CY followed by the new setting.

Random Indicators
Under this system there was no external indication of the use of the random indicators system.

Wahlworts
Any non-textual word or phrase used at the beginning or end of a cipher, used to avoid stereotyped beginnings or endings.

Mosse Code
A book of code groups, based on a commercial code compiled by Rudolph Mosse of Hamburg before the war, but developed and expanded during the war. It substituted semi-pronounceable five-letter groups for common words or phrases, thus LUFTGAU became GELIP.

Double Encoding
By a change of encoding procedure, to use, without danger, a key believed to be compromised, but which could not be immediately replaced.

There is also a summary, from Bletchley Park's point of view, on how the Germans could have overcome some of the problems associated with the Enigma cipher machine, as well as general observations on cipher security learned from German mistakes made during the war.
It is assumed that the reader has a general knowledge of how an Enigma cipher machine works.

General

Between January 1944 and May 1945 the Germans introduced a large number of security measures. Some were W/T camouflage and had their effect on cryptology in that they made proper traffic identification more difficult. Other measures were essentially cryptographic, i.e., they affected the actual process of encoding and thus influenced BP's methods of breaking. There were broadly three groups:

(a) mechanical gadgets which involved the provision of an addition to the standard Enigma machine;
(b) alteration of the key;
(c) encoding rules

The separate devices adopted were: Reflector D, Enigma Uhr, Zusatz stecker, NOT-Schlüssel, CY, Random Indicators, Wahlworts, the Mosse Code and Double Encoding.
These new devices were of very unequal importance. Technically, D and Uhr were far more important than the rest, and D was much more serious than the rest put together. Class (b) was a minor nuisance, while class (c) did not fundamentally affect breaking methods, but did make breaking more difficult.
While the German security drive of 1944 was on a more thorough scale than previously, some of the devices had been used earlier or were on the lines of measures previously adopted.

Reflector D

Uncle D, as it was affectionately known, was a household word in Hut 6 from January 1944 to the end of the war, and was primarily a German Air Force (GAF) security device. Up to and including July 1944, D was confined to the GAF general operational key, called Red at Bletchley Park. From August onwards its range was extended and consequently the number of Ds recovered rose rapidly. From January to July, 21 of these were recovered, but from August to the end of the war 379 – including just over 100 by capture.

The first menace

On 23 December 1943, Hut 6 received an unwelcome jolt. A Red message was intercepted from Norway, which gave instructions that a new reflector – called Umkehrwalze Dora – was to come into force on 1 January 1944. It was not clear whether the new reflector was to be used on part of the Red system, or on all of it. Preparations were made that Red as a whole might go over to the new reflector and thus, at a stroke, become unbreakable by BP's normal method – the Bombe.

Hut 6 was then suddenly faced with the possibility of a first-class cryptographic crisis which was liable to result in the loss for an indefinite time of the principal GAF key – Red – the cornerstone of all Air cryptography and still at the top of the intelligence ladder. If it came into universal use, it would (until broken) make all the hundreds of Bombes so much waste metal.

Meanwhile, preparations were made in the last week of 1943 for the worst, i.e., that Red would go over wholly to D. At the time there was only one way to tackle the problem – to break by the SKO (Stecker (plugboard) Knock-Out – a means of determining the stecker of an Enigma key) method on a long crib (the plain language equivalent of a stretch of cipher text) – which could probably only be attained by a re-encodement from some other key.

Perhaps no single day in Hut 6 history was more memorable than its own D-Day, New Year's Day 1944.

The first break was that of Leek – an Eastern Europe weather key – at 1100, followed by the vital break of Red at 1150. Later that day, it became clear that messages on the Norwegian Auto (an automatic transmitting set) and some on the GHQ Auto were not coming out. A reasonable beginner (a crib used at the beginning of a message) – SEQSXFREDX – was then rodded (an Enigma-breaking system) on one of the Norwegian messages, assuming the Red stecker, wheel order and ringstellung (which gave the turnover on the rods).

What was obviously the correct story was discovered, but there was no hole through the Jeffreys sheets (which recorded, by punched holes, the electrical connections between the reflector and the two left-hand wheels), therefore the presence of a new reflector was proved. The rodding was then continued through the middle wheel and the wiring of the reflector was established by Oliver Lawn at 0130 on the morning of 2 January.

The BO mystery

Bombes, hand machines and Decoding Room machines were fitted with the new reflector, and in the first week of January 1944 at least one Red key was broken on a crib run on D. The D traffic did not come out on the wiring already known. A new wiring was recovered which had one pairing only – BO – common with the first D. This showed that D was a many-sided device. Every 10 days a new D came into force on Red and every D had the common pairing BO.

Argument turned principally on the significance to be attached to the fixed pairing BO, but it was by no means clear what theory this peculiarity supported. The pluggable theory was proved correct by the capture of the Red key-sheet for June 1944 with the D pairings on it. To remove all doubt, the column containing these pairings was headed:

STECKERVERBINDUNGEN AN DEN UMKEHRWALZE

The D pairings were written vertically in three columns of four pairings each. For the month there were three Ds, each covering approximately ten days. There were 12 variable pairings and the fixed pairing BO.

Greenshank and D

Then it was discovered that Greenshank – the key of the 20 military administrative districts (Wehrkreise) of Greater Germany – and the prize of prizes for Hut 6 Army Research, was using a new reflector or a new wheel. The possibility remained of a break by SKO, and one of the great personal triumphs of Hut 6 – the break of Greenshank of 27 April 1944 – on a re-encodement of some 200 letters, was obtained. This feat was effected in about a week. This break made it highly probable that Greenshank was using D, as the BO pairing appeared, and this supposition was confirmed by later Greenshank breaks in 1945.

Meanwhile, the Red Ds were being broken regularly and with no great difficulty. There was some uncertainty about when the second and third Ds of the month would come into force, but this caused little serious trouble in practice. Hut 6 constructed suitable tables and invented the 'Half-Enigma' (a type of hand machine in which the terminals of the reflector may be connected direct to the lampboard).

BP, however, could not always rely on the Germans making the mistake of using both reflector B (the standard reflector) and D on the same key – sooner or later there would be a great extension of the use of D. Most attention was paid to mechanical D-breaking devices. Of them all, **Duenna** – a machine invented by American experts – proved most successful. At last it became apparent that something was going to happen on 1 August – Hut 6's second D-Day.

By 2 August three distinct Ds had been broken – disproving the pleasing illusion that all keys might share a common D. There was no significant extension in the use of D on Red, and at least five keys were free from D. There was also no appearance of D on Army keys. However, Wasp, the key of Fliegerkorps IX, went over wholly to D on 5 August.

From later evidence and BP's general knowledge of the GAF Cipher Office it appears that, prior to August 1944, only the Red key sheet had Ds printed on it. It was believed that in the GAF cipher office a number of keys were made up, and then the key number and discriminants (which indicated the key being used) added in a fixed order which determined the nature of each key. On this theory, not until the discriminants were added was the nature of the key known.

Thus, before August 1944, the Red D must have been made up when the discriminants were added, and not when the key was composed. But from August on, it is simplest to suppose that every key, when made up, had its quota of Ds added before the keys were identified by number and discriminants.

On this theory it follows that from August 1944 every GAF key had a set of Ds attached, i.e., every key was liable to use D. But it does not follow that every key did use D. First, certain units might not have D distributed to them. Second, even if an operator had D, there is a lot of evidence to show that D was so unpopular with German cipher clerks that they would not use it without explicit and repeated orders. The long-term effects of the extension of D from August until the end of the war, was a steady increase in the difficulty of breaking most GAF keys.

First, the problem of recovering the D even when the rest of the key was known was no longer the formality it had been on Red, which was a large key with at most times a plethora of reasonable cribs – most other keys were in a less happy state. Various ingenious methods of breaking a D on a known key without a crib were devised. The first occasion was in September when a key was broken by 'Bobbery', invented by Robert Roseveare, a method of recovering D wirings when the wheel order, ringstellung and stecker of the key were known, but no crib was available on a message encoded with D. Special problems were provided by 'nearly D' or 'wholly D' keys. A 'nearly D' key was one on which the bulk of the traffic and all, or most of the best cribs, were habitually on D. It was necessary, on these keys, to secure an entry on a B crib – not an easy task as they were by definition inferior or fewer – or on a stray B re-encodement.

D-breaks

D-breaking machines were constructed both in the UK and America, and no sooner were they in working order than their services were called for on operational jobs, and Hut 6 was compelled by sheer necessity to use highly complicated machinery which was still in an experimental stage.

Giant – an ingenious makeshift comprising four Bombes designed to recover unknown reflector wirings, was the hero of the early days, but demanded a crib of 200 letters.

The **Autoscritcher** (an American-designed machine for recovering unknown reflector wirings) was not ready until the last few months of the war, but in a short working life showed its merits.

Duenna, the steadiest and most successful machine, began working operationally in December 1944, and was joined in a few months by a sister machine and further reinforced by a third sister towards the end. In the closing months of the war came the capture of many key sheets with their accompanying Ds. A large number of these were Ds Hut 6 would never have broken on its own. The dates when new Ds came into force showed considerable variation. From November 1944 on, every key had four Ds a month as opposed to the earlier three. In September and October the practice varied strangely from key to key.

Summary of the German use of D

On cipher security of D, the German cardinal error sticks out a mile. It was a capital blunder for the Germans to have 'mixed keys' using both B and D. Any individual key should have been wholly D or not to have used it at all. It is the more surprising that the Germans made this error as the Army – which must have used D on Greenshank in 1943 – used the device correctly. The GAF cipher authorities adopted and misused the excellent invention of the Army. D should have been considered an integral part of the key, not an extra.

The effect of a sudden wholesale introduction of D on to selected keys would have been a much more crushing blow to Hut 6 than the slow and piecemeal changes that the Germans preferred. In warfare, a new weapon should be first employed in massive strength, not in penny numbers.

Zusatz Stecker

In May 1944 the Germans introduced the most silly and trivial of their security devices, and yet the forewarning BP received of their intention to do so caused considerable fluttering of the dovecotes. The reason was that the decode references to the impending change were – from BP's viewpoint – very cryptic. What was abundantly clear was that on any one day, three different sets of stecker were to be in use on any one key. Hut 6 prepared for the worst.

This would mean that every key would have to be broken three times over, indefinitely, except for the second and third breaks, when one would presumably know the wheel order and ringstellung and could run on hoppity (a type of Bombe or menu designed to allow for successive turnover assumptions, made possible by a knowledge of the position of the right-hand ringstellung clip) menus, which meant shorter cribs. This possibility was in one way providential as there were few, if any keys, where BP could have produced, every day in the relevant periods, three full-dress cribs.

However, Hut 6 were faced with the necessity of a great expansion of its records, as they might have had to use, as cribs, beginners or signatures which it had previously despised and left unrecorded. An enlarged scheme of records was set on foot and all embryo cribs were carefully noted.

A damp squib

What happened was an anti-climax. The Germans changed the stecker at 0300, 1500 and 2300, giving three stecker periods called by Hut 6 R, S and T. In combination with the already existing wheel order periods, X, Y and Z, the 24 hours from 0300 to 0300 were now divided into five key periods: 0300-1059 RX, 1100-1449 RY, 1500-1859 SY, 1900-2259 SZ and 2300-0259 TZ. Each set of stecker consisted, as usual, of 10 stecker pairs plus six self-stecker, but at 1500 one of the original stecker pairs was unsteckered and two of the originally self-steckered letters were steckered together. At 2300 the same process was repeated with another of the original 10 stecker pairs and two more letters of the original six self-stecker, e.g., Red for 1 May 1944:

R	A/E	B/Y	D/G	F/J	H/L	K/O	M/R	P/U	S/X	T/V	C I N Q W Z
S	A/E	B/Y	D/G	F/J	H/L	I/Z	K/O	M/R	S/X	T/V	C N P Q U W
T	A/E	B/Y	F/J	H/L	I/Z	K/O	M/R	N/Q	S/X	T/V	C D G P U W

It is obvious that the alteration in the stecker is so slight that it is, in general, a fairly simple matter – with some knowledge of cribs or even without – to deduce the other two sets from any given set. Serious difficulty only arose when traffic in one period was very small. Thus it was not always possible on certain keys to recover the T stecker. It is surprising that the Germans thought such a trivial alteration gave any additional cipher security worth bothering about.

Extent of change
The Army, characteristically, had nothing to do with this half-baked innovation, but Zusatz Stecker was employed by all Air keys until about 15 June 1944, when it was dropped generally as suddenly as it came into use. The abandonment was hailed with jubilation by all concerned as Zusatz Stecker had become simply a time-wasting nuisance.

It is difficult to suggest any really satisfactory and adequate motive for the German introduction of this paltry nuisance. It may be suggested that it is in line with the remarkable German nervousness over depth (e.g., change of wheel order), and in particular that it was introduced as a stop-gap until Enigma Uhr, a more radical stecker change idea, was ready.

Zusatz Stecker can scarcely have been born in the brain of a professional cryptographer. It is not improbable that the Germans themselves gave it up in disgust, eventually realising that such a futile key-change was not even worth the trouble it caused to their own operators.

Enigma Uhr

The problem
With Enigma Uhr, the Germans, for once, sprang a complete surprise on BP. On 10 July 1944, on Jaguar, the key of Luftflotte 3 (later Luftwaffen Kdo. West), certain messages began with a number, which ran from 1 to 39, and then went off into nonsense. Also, a decode referred to one of these messages as enciphered with 'Enigma Uhr'. It was clear that the nonsense represented an additional re-encoding of some kind on top of the normal Enigma, almost certainly performed by a mechanical gadget.

The first step in solving this problem was clearly to break into one of the Uhr messages and this would have been by no means easy had not the Fusion Room – the department of the traffic analysis body, Sixta, the Hut 6 section responsible for collation and distribution of information relevant to cryptographic, intelligence and W/T sections – been able to produce a re-encipherment between a 'plain' Enigma message and an Uhr message. This re-encipherment led to the breaking of the first Uhr substitution – a reciprocal stecker different from the basic stecker. The episode was one of the most tense in the history of Hut 6.

Extension of Uhr

Uhr was always an Air gadget and never used by the Army. Originally used by two keys, it was later extended to 15 Air keys. Uhr alone had little influence on the breaking of keys. In running on the Bombe, Uhr created no serious difficulties in principle, for it was possible, by using closures only, to allow for the probable non-reciprocity of the stecker. But, longer cribs were required, and this meant that a key which used Uhr very extensively and had rather short cribs, was made more difficult to break. But, if long cribs or re-encodements were available, Uhr was not a major cryptographic obstacle.

Uhr notation

The Germans originally indicated the Uhr number by encoding it with the basic key at the beginning of the message, but later a method of encoding the number was introduced by which the number was represented by four letters encoded in the basic key at the start of the message according to a simple bigram code.

The manner in which this new notation was discovered is interesting. On Jaguar of November 1944 there were some inexplicable duds (failed to decode). It was thought these might be on a separate key, but several cribs failed. Fortunately, someone had the bright idea that the message might be on Jaguar Uhr, with a new method of indicating the number, and a message was tried on all 40 sets of stecker. It came out on 28 and showed up the four dummy letters and the rest was easy. So, but for an inspired guess, Hut 6 might not have discovered this new notation for several days. Once discovered, on balance the change helped, although it made the recovering of the basic key from an initial Uhr break more difficult. However, it simplified running on an Uhr message, as the message had to begin in the fifth place.

A captured document on Enigma Uhr showed that this second notation was that originally intended by the Germans. They made a great security mistake in adopting the inferior method of starting off with the number encoded in the basic key, as this drew attention to the problem, and told BP that some transformation of the Jaguar stecker was the answer. The Germans, by departing from the explicit instructions of the devisers of this gadget, greatly weakened its security value.

Summary

Enigma Uhr was a highly ingenious device, and was regarded by the Germans as increasing markedly the security of Enigma, but they made two mistakes. Had they concentrated the use of Uhr more – e.g., had they made Jaguar, the key where they used it most, an all-Uhr key – and had they used the alphabetical notation from the start, they would have made BP's initial Uhr break much more difficult. As so often, the Germans' piecemeal methods were their ruin. Even so, Enigma Uhr was a highly complicated and intricate device, but which, from the security angle, did not come within a thousand miles of the mechanically much simpler Reflector D.

To make Enigma Uhr a really dangerous device – which would have upset BP's breaking technique – its basic principle of stecker transformation should have been carried further. For example, if the Uhr had been used in every message and made to move on one position for each letter encoded, it would have given rise to a cycle of 40 stecker sets inside every message. It would have involved radical changes to the Bombe design, if not the invention of wholly new machines.

NOT-Schlüssel

Introduction

The use of NOT-Schlüssel (emergency keys) is, as a security measure, not quite in the same category as those already discussed. The object was not to render cryptography more difficult, but to give a quick method of distributing new keys in case of compromise, particularly to isolated garrisons. The method adopted was to devise a system by which an Enigma key could be generated by a single keyword while the discriminant was found from another word. The two words could be selected from an emergency list held in reserve or, in case of need, sent over the air in Enigma. This last procedure was most insecure as the German instructions had been captured, and so BP could devise the key from the key word as well as the Germans could.

First system

The first system was explained in two documents that came into BP's hands in August 1944. The procedure is best described by an example: Let the keyword (schlüsselwort) be OSTSEEFISCH (C H, C K are not to be replaced by Q as was usual in Enigma messages – also an umlaut is ignored). First, strike out all but the first example of any repeated letter giving the "fillet" OSTEFICH. Then write underneath this fillet in alphabetical order all the other letters of the alphabet thus:

```
6 7 8 2 3 5 1 4
O S T E F I C H
A B D G J K L M
N P Q R U V W X
Y Z
```

and (as shown) number the letters in the fillet alphabetically. Then read off the letters by columns, in the numbered order, and arrange them to form a rectangle 13 x 2, thus:

```
C L W E G R F J U H M X I
K V O A N Y S B P Z T D Q
4     1 5         2       3
```

Number from 1 to 5 the five letters in the bottom row that come earliest in the alphabet and then read off the key thus:

Wheelorder:	4 1 5 (the first three numbers from the left)
Ringstellung	C E G (the letters of the top row above those numbered letters that give the wheelorder)
Stecker pairs:	L/V W/O R/Y F/S J/B U/P H/Z M/T X/D I/Q

All the normal key rules disappear. In particular, consecutive stecker are impossible.

There is, however, one way of identifying a broken key as NOT – the (German) ringstellung involves letters that are self-steckered. (This one can be used as a short cut to the ringstellung of a NOT-key).

The discriminant of a NOT-key is obtained from the Kenngruppenwort (discriminant) by using the 1st, 3rd and 5th letters. There is thus only one discriminant a key and stutters (a trigram having a repeated letter such as JJM, JJJ or JMJ – used of a discriminant) are quite possible.

Guernsey saga and the Forty NOTS

NOT-keys were used by 'General der L.W. Kanalinseln', whose HQ was in Germany and who was completely cut off, having to constantly use emergency keys. A list of the discriminant cycle from 1 September to 10 October 1944 is shown below. The discriminants from 1 to 5 September are bracketed, as no traffic was passed on these keys, but these are the discriminants that would have been used:

Sept		Sept		Sept		Oct	
1	(OEN)	11	HSL	21	FIC	1	HSL
2	(TAE)	12	ASR	22	KSM	2	ASR
3	(PED)	13	TBK	23	LPO	3	TBK
4	(KKO)	14	BGE	24	EHB	4	BGE
5	(TAS)	15	NBN	25	BHS	5	NBN
6	TBK	16	PRE	26	DEK	6	PRE
7	ASH	17	NRL	27	TCR	7	NRL
8	TEN	18	OTE	28	TIH	8	OTE
9	HRE	19	NMO	29	ERH	9	NMO
10	DNN	20	DNN	30	TAC	10	RNG

In this unimpressive list of trigrams is locked the secret of the forty NOTS. The keywords from 8 to 10 September were given as follows:

Schlüsselwort	*Kenngruppenwort*
8 Ostseefisch	Trennschnitt
9 Nimrod	Harfe
0 Randgebiet	Duenenlandschaft

This was the beginning of Hut 6 building up the series of 'forty code words'. Some other keys were also broken on re-encipherments and NOT/ASH, with its codeword NORDLICHT, was already known. The situation became steadily more complicated. First, it became clear that the "one discriminant, one key" theory was not universally true. It will be noticed that up to 30 September there are two cases of repeated discriminants in the list, namely TBK on 6 and 13 September, DNN on 10 and 20 September. Now, on 10 and 20 September, the same key decoded all the traffic. It did not decode anyone else's TBK traffic. It was fortunately possible to disprove the theory that the key TBK had been worked out wrongly by the Germans, for we were able to recover the generating word PFERDEKOPPEL (= paddock).

In October the mystery deepened. As will have been noticed, the discriminant from 1 to 9 October traffic did not come out on the September keys, several of which had been broken. Fortunately, BP were quickly able to break NOT-Guernsey of 4 October on a re-encipherment from Raster (a hand cipher which replaced Double Playfair as the type of non-machine cipher most closely associated in use and content with Enigma). The General continued to use a Raster key in happy ignorance that it was already at Bletchley Park. The key was found to be completely different from the NOT/BGE key used on 14 September. Once again BP tried to break the keyword and soon arrived at the fillet ENHOBAK, which did not look like any German word. However, about the same time there was a somewhat obscure message finally translated as follows:

> *Key message from 1/10 0300 hours*
> *Kenngruppennworte as Schluesselworte, read backwards,*
> *beginning with Laufende Nr. 1. Kenngruppen*
> *from the Schluesselworte, read forwards.*

With this hint of reading backwards the fillet was reversed to read KABOHNE. This suggested KAKAOBOHNE, which read forward gave the fillet KAOBHNE (which generated the key of 14 September) and read backwards the fillet ENHOBAK (note that the fillet from a backward word is not necessarily a backward fillet) – which generated the key of 4 October. Also, KAKAOBOHNE is clearly one of the original discriminant words – see KKO on 4 September.

It was by this time clear that the General had been given a list of 10 pairs of code words which he had used straight from 1-10 September and afterwards in several varied ways. It is possible to derive 40 keys from 10 pairs of words by using each word in turn as the keyword and using it first forwards and then backwards. The General's scheme was soon discovered to be as follows, if the original Schlüsselwort is denoted by S and the original Kenngruppenwort by K:

	Schlüsselwort	*Kenngruppenwort*
1-10 September	S forwards	K forwards
11-20 September	K forwards	S forwards
21-30 September	S backwards	K backwards

(from No. 10 to 1)

It was possible to deduce the scheme up to 10 October from the keys already broken, and the scheme from the 11th to the 20th was given to BP in a message of the 10th. Only 40 keys are possible and are all used in the period 1 September to 10 October, so, in order to have NOT-Guernsey out until the General got a new set of words, BP had merely to find the 40 code words.

A number were already known by analysis from the keys and from source, but the attack was now pressed forward more systematically. It was now much easier to find the keyword for broken keys, for in every case BP could say "the discriminant formed from the keyword for which we are looking is (say) TAE, therefore the word is T.A.E…" In this way, keyword after keyword was discovered and more and more keys written out.

It was also possible to discover keywords even when the key had not been broken. For example on 25 September the discriminant was BHS and on 5 September TAS. Hence the generating word must be T.A.S………..S.H.B., the central dots representing an unknown number of letters. Another skeleton crossword clue was A.S.H………R.C.T. Both of these were solved by fortunate inspirations and the aid of dictionaries, and BP were ultimately successful in hammering out the complete list which is as follows:

FINAL LIST OF KEYWORDS AND DISCRIMINANT WORDS

Lfd. Nr.	Schlüsselwort	Kenngruppenwort
1	HASELRUTE	OZEASCHIFF
2	ANSTRICHFARBE	TRAUERMUSIK
3	TABAKPFEIPE	PFERDEKOPPEL
4	BAGGERSCHIFF	KAKAOBOHNE
5	NEBENHAUS	TRANSPORTNACHSCHUB
6	PFRIEM	TABAKFELD
7	NORDLICHT	ANSCHAUUNGSUNTERRICH
8	OSTSEEFISCH	TRENNSCHNITT
9	NIMROD	HARFE
10	RANDGEBIET	DUNENLANDSCHAFT

This list clears up the mystery of the two TBK keys referred to above, as there are two words that give the discriminant TRK.

New-style NOT-keys
In December 1944 the Germans gave full details of a new style of NOT-keys in a document. This was definitely an improvement – a pair of code-words gave keys for a month, and yet there was perfect security, as the codeword was virtually unbreakable from a given key.

Conclusions
The two systems of constructing NOT-keys were equally ingenious, but the second was preferable on security grounds as it gave a month's keys from a pair of words while keeping the codewords inviolate. These systems were only intended for use in emergencies. NOT-keys had the fatal objection for regular use that, if the actual key is generated from one word, the number of possible keys is limited so drastically that some kind of key index becomes possible.
The regular use of any system of deriving keys from key-words could never be secure unless two conditions were satisfied:

1. that the method adopted did not, in itself, give rise to any peculiarity or rule in the keys; and
2. that the number of possible keys was not substantially reduced by the method of derivation. In practice, to satisfy the second condition, it would be necessary to derive each key from more than one keyword.

C Y

Introduction:
About the middle of September 1944 a new German security device was noticed, in which a number of messages went off into nonsense in the middle and this always happened just after the decode read CY followed by two consecutive letters, e.g., RS. The left-hand wheel could be decoded if, immediately after CYRS, the left-hand wheel was set to the first of the two consecutive letters (in this case R). While the consecutive letters were not always the same, the CY was invariable.

Apart from a few messages, CY was purely an Army idea. It was later discovered that the Police key – Roulette – was the first key to use CY, and was in practically universal use on all Army and SS keys except on short messages.

Effect on breaking
The most important result of CY was that it effectively ruled out cillying (a cilli was a means to use the end position of one message as the outside indicator of the next), which was now (if it occurred at all) very hard to spot. Whether from this cause or from the concomitant introduction of random indicators, cillying virtually ceased on Army traffic and SS keys, a loss that would have been more serious had not cillies already been very rare (except on the SS key Orange).

Other difficulties were that the insertion of the four dummy letters at an unknown spot upset cribs – particularly top and tail shots – and more especially re-encodements.

It was a help to BP that they had a copy of the German regulations so that they knew when to expect CY, and most cribs did not run into the danger zone. Greenshank re-encipherments were especially affected as (because of the presence of D) it was necessary to write out at the very least 80 letters correctly and (even apart from CY) this was by no means easy. Yet it is surprising how often these difficulties were overcome. In one minor aspect CY was an advantage. On occasion – particularly when a day came out on the beginning of a message – it provided a shortcut to the ringstellung, which was often taken advantage of by Army cryptographers.

Conclusion
CY was basically a device for removing (if only to a slight degree) one of the main theoretical defects of the Enigma – the extreme regularity of its wheel motion. In default of a mechanical method of producing a more irregular motion (the Germans had planned to introduce this later), the idea of breaking the continual uniformity by an unpredictable change once in each message is not without merit, although it was essentially only a makeshift.

Random Indicators

Introduction
Under this system there was no external indication of the use of the random indicators system, but from various small scraps of evidence it was not unlikely that it was used fairly extensively, at least on Army and SS keys. The evidence is:

(1) These keys used CY punctiliously and thus might be expected to use the companion devices.

(2) The sudden cessation of cillies on Orange (an SS key) and (to a lesser degree) Roulette (the Senior Police key) is most easily explained by random indicators (in the case of Orange at least CY is not adequate in itself. In August 1944 long strings of keyboards had appeared and the use of CY will not conceal an absolutely first class cilli story, though it will camouflage a weak one).

(3) The fairly frequent use of repeated indicators on Army keys is best explained by inadvertent breaches of one of the rules.

(4) The actual use of the device is proved by the capture of at least one Enigma set-up with wheelorder 1 2 3, ringstellung A A A (German) – and by the later capture of more than one Spruchschlüsselliste.

Conclusion
It is impossible to interpret 'Random Indicators' as anything but an anti-cilli device – a far more radical one than CY. It did kill cillies and the Germans had at least become conscious of this possible danger. The answer they found to the danger of cillies was as effective as anything that could have been devised – short of a complete change of the indicating system – and it did lose BP Orange. The only possible criticism of the German action is that (as so often) it was too late. Cillies were dying when they were killed. The history of Hut 6 would have been different had the Germans, in the full flush of their 1940 triumphs, been able to spare a thought for the suppression of cillies.

Wahlworts

Introduction
A wahlwort (the German word quickly became naturalised in Hut 6 parlance and the attempt to introduce 'nonsense word' as an English equivalent never caught on) is a word, chosen at random by the encoder of a message and placed at the beginning or end, for the sole purpose of defeating enemy cryptographers. The first occurrence of wahlworts was on the African Army keys (the Finches) in December 1942. Early that month the Germans sent in Chaffinch a strong anti-crib warning to the effect that:

1 addresses and signatures were to be buried in messages, preceded by a warning signal, e.g., 'Here follows address'; and

2 addresses (if of standard length) were to be altered by the prefixing of nonsense words.

Long before the month was out, the second instruction had been carried into effect (the proviso being disregarded), and a plague of wahlworts had infected all the African keys with the providential exception of Phoenix, the key of Panzerarmee Afrika. The effect on the breaking position was immediately serious, and for two reasons it produced a much greater impact on the Hut as a whole.

Firstly, the keys concerned were among the most important operational keys then being broken. They could not be laid aside if necessary (as could be done to a certain extent with wahlwort-ridden keys later on), and hence the increased Bombe time they required had an immediate effect on the fortunes of other keys. Secondly, Bombe resources were still so limited that a prolonged crisis of this nature might (and at its worst moments did) rule out running of Research jobs altogether, a result that would not have been arrived at had a similar crisis occurred a year later when BP had more Bombes here as well as American resources.

Extension of wahlworts

Wahlworts were never used on SS keys and until the closing months of the war were mainly an Army device, and if a certain key at a certain time used wahlworts, this did not mean that every message on the key had a wahlwort. On Army keys, from December 1942 to the end of the campaign in May 1943, wahlworts were freely and widely used on all African Army keys except Phoenix.

But during the rest of 1943 it became clear – that in theory at least – the use of wahlworts was a general Army security measure. There was hardly any Army key that might not use wahlworts.

In the last year of the war, wahlworts were very fortunately not used to a predominant extent on Western Army keys with the exception of the general key Puffin. However, the Eastern and Balkan keys had become more and more addicted to wahlworts, and by the end of the war, wahlworts were fairly universal on Army keys. Greenshank, however, was to the end a distinguished exception. A few Air keys used wahlworts from an early date, but generally remained free of them until the closing months of the war.

Use of wahlworts

The usual practice was to use wahlworts at the beginning and end of each message, i.e., in part messages the wahlworts were at the beginning of the first part and the end of the last part. Occasionally, a more radical method was adopted by which wahlworts were used at the beginning and end of every part. It was fortunate that this extension of the practice was not universally adopted.

The length of the wahlworts might vary considerably and it was an important part of crib records to note each encoder's favourite length and hence to fix the limits within which cribs should be staggered. As a general rule, four to 14 letters was normal. Rare alike were wahlworts of three letters and the freaks of about 40. Two of the latter deserve to be handed down to the admiration of posterity. The first is the classic:

DONAUDAMPSSQUIFFAHRTGESELLSQAFTSKAPITAEN

and the other is the remarkable tongue-twister:

HOTTENTOTENPOTENTATENTANTENATTENTAETER

This can be translated as "would-be-murderers-of-the-Hottentot-potentates'-aunts". The wahlwort might – and often was – immediately followed by the text of the message proper. However, some form of punctuation such as X or YY could be inserted. In the last month of the war it became the rule on both Air and Army keys to mark out the wahlwort clearly by doubling the last two letters of the initial wahlwort and the first two letters of the final wahlwort and (assuming no intermediate punctuation) it was possible to use this doubling in making up menus. Thus, on Avocet II – key of the Army High Command – which was often broken on GEHEIMEKOMMANDOSAQE (TOP SECRET), staggered (to try a crib at a number of consecutive positions of the message) to allow for an initial wahlwort. GEHEIMEKOMMANDOSAQE could then be run, secure in the knowledge that each pair of queries would represent the same letter.

On the choice of wahlworts, in theory this should have been purely random – in practice it was not. Nouns were almost invariably chosen. Individual operators had their favourite wahlworts, and some, e.g., SOMMER, WINTER and HUNGER occurred again and again. Sometimes the initial and final wahlworts in a message were connected in a sense, e.g., MUSIK … TANZ, or in some other way there was an obvious appropriateness. But, in general, such peculiarities were not sufficiently consistent to be predictable and hence usable. There was one instructive exception to this rule.

One operator became so attached to the wahlworts Guten … Morgen, Guten … Abend (each at the appropriate time of day), that it was reckoned at one time, that it was better than an even chance that these wahlworts were correct.

Effect on breaking

Such an exceptional tour de force, however, cannot outweigh the generally prejudicial effect of wahlworts on BP's success. It is evident that at best, i.e., when one has good cribs, the introduction of wahlworts might have meant the running of three or four versions instead of one. With poor cribs that have several variant forms, the case was still worse. Thus the thorough use of wahlworts would, on almost any key, make breaking more expensive in time and on a key with a weak crib position may have made it unbreakable except at extravagant cost.

Value of wahlworts

In wahlworts the Germans hit on a simple and effective method of making cribbing more difficult. It would have been still more effective but for the eternal German blunder of 'too little and too late'. Introduced in 1940 on a wholesale scale, wahlworts might have knocked out the infant Hut 6 Crib Room before it had got properly on its feet. But the Germans did not use the system at all until halfway through the war, and not until the last few months did they use it on anything approaching a universal scale. The rival system (used on Roulette) of burying addresses and signatures in the middle of the message was perhaps preferable, although much depended on the nature of the traffic. Best of all such methods was the radical device of the cut. By this, any message was arbitrarily divided into two parts and the second part encoded first. This simple but effective proceeding made cribbing quite impossible, except perhaps in the case of short messages, where the complete text could be guessed. In wahlworts the Germans discovered a useful weapon against cribbery – but not a complete answer.

The Mosse Code

The Mosse Code – named after its author, Rudolf Mosse – was invented before the war as a purely commercial code. The code-words were adopted by the GAF and given new meanings. It was used on Air keys – never on Army and SS keys – from early 1944 onwards, but it was not until 1945 that (in consequence of certain changes in its nature) it became a factor of some importance as an anti-crib measure. In origin it probably was not intended as such, but was meant (like most internal codes in a cipher) to secure brevity in encoding and perhaps to serve as a measure of internal security. The meanings of some of the codewords were soon discovered from their context, but in September 1944, Hut 3 was able to publish, from captured documents, the complete code as used in March. It then consisted of about 500 five-letter codewords, the vast majority denoting individual units or commands in the GAF. Even then, a few codewords represented recurrent phrases, e.g.,

PAPIC = FEHLANZEIGE

It was this element that was destined to become more pronounced. In 1945 the code was largely altered and its character changed.

It was again possible to build it up from messages, and in April 1945 there was published a final revised list of the reconstructed code.

It still consisted – as always – of five-letter codewords, but now a far greater number stood for recurrent phrases as opposed to formations of the GAF. A few selected examples follow:

```
FLYMI = FEHLANZEIGE
GUFWY = VOLLZUGSMELDUNG
JERRO = TAGESABSCHLUSSMELDUNG
JIJUS = ABENDMELDUNG
NEPER = EINSATZBEREITSCHAFTSMELDUNG
ORHAF = LUFTLAGEBERICHT
```

In addition, dates, times and numbers could be represented by words beginning with T, U and Z respectively. Whether by deliberate intention or not, Mosse certainly discovered a sound security measure. It can be readily understood that the replacement of EINSATZBEREITSCHAFTSMELDUNG by NEPER (while technically merely the substitution of one crib for another) is decidedly a change for the worse, for, given reasonable consistency of form, the value of a crib depends on its length. Whether by deliberate intention or not, Mosse certainly discovered a sound security measure. Indeed, the replacement of regularly occurring phrases by brief codewords (preferably a range of alternative codewords for each phrase) must always be regarded as a useful ancillary to more radical anti-crib precautions. Yet, on the other hand, some cribs were actually improved by the use of the Mosse Code. This happened when several alternative abbreviations were replaced by the standard codeword.

Double encoding

Double encoding, in contra-distinction to the devices already described, was essentially provisional in nature. The object was apparently, by a change of encoding procedure, to use, without danger, a key believed to be compromised but which, for some reason, could not be immediately replaced. It was a cumbrous procedure and very laborious to the Germans.

Hence, it is not surprising that it was used on only two keys – Raven (key of Heeresgruppe E) and Gadfly (key of Luftwaffen Kdo. Süd Ost) – and in each case on only a small portion of the traffic. Raven only used the device on a single day – 16 March 1944 – at least so far as Hut 6 were aware.

Raven: Double encoding on Raven was revealed by a fortunate reference in another message on the same day, and by an examination of the duds, a few doubly encoded messages were found. These messages had to be decoded in two stages. First, one found the message setting in the usual way and decoded the Enigma text. This came out apparently still in Enigma (as indeed it was), but the first 12 letters had the pattern ABC ABC DEF DEF. The next step was to treat ABC DEF as a new preamble, find the message setting and then decode the rest of the message starting at this setting. The encoding method must be obvious from the above account of the converse process.

Gadfly: The method used here on was somewhat different. It gave rise to apparent duds. But, to the credit of Hut 6, the solution was discovered by the Chief Cryptographer before it was revealed by a full explanation in a message. The method is best explained from the encoder's standpoint.

The encoder chose his message setting – say A B C – and enciphered his message in the normal way. Let us assume the message is 234 letters long and he consequently ends at A K C. (We take it that neither wheel 2 nor 4 is in the middle). Then, without moving the wheels, the operator proceeds to encode gain in Enigma the already encoded cipher text.

For the encoder this is simple enough, if twice as laborious as usual. For the decoder, matters are much more difficult. In the normal way he finds the setting A B C, then he must determine the closing position A K C either by calculation in Hut 6-style or by the German-recommended method, unutterably tedious but foolproof, of tapping out the message. Having discovered A K C, he then decodes the Enigma text to Enigma text and then has to decode this with the original setting A B C, truly a case of "Double, double, toil and trouble" if ever there was one!

To complete the subject, it is possible, with a little ingenuity, to run a crib on a doubly encoded message (Gadfly-style). Assume, for instance, there is a crib starting TAGESMELDUNG VOM and that the length of the message is 234 as above – then, in the simplest case, if the doubly encoded Enigma text is P X Z C P … … then there is a menu starting:

T   ZZA   ?   ZIA   P   ZID   ?   ZZD   E

Thus query menus can be built up. These have to be run to allow for all probable turnover assumptions, so the whole process is by no means inexpensive. Yet this method was on several occasions successful in securing breaks.

Summary and Conclusions

General

From the practical standpoint, it is certainly possible to construct an unbreakable Enigma. What follows is an attempt to analyse the general concept of cipher security with illustrations from the Enigma and then to explain why the Germans so signally failed to attain it.

First, to deal with the subject on general lines. Two assumptions only are made:

(1) That the cipher system is high-grade, i.e. intended to resist cryptographic assault indefinitely.

(2) That the enemy cryptographer knows the construction of the permanent elements in the cipher system, i.e. in the case of a machine cipher, the elements of the machine that cannot be changed every day are assumed known. In the special case of the German Enigma as used by the GAF and Army, there is postulated a knowledge of the wiring of wheels 1 to 5 and of Reflector B.

This second assumption is that Hut 6 possessed this knowledge from October 1939 and in warfare it is fairly certain that sooner or later the enemy will capture any machine that is used extensively. Hence no machine is secure unless messages enciphered by it are still unbreakable even after the machine has been captured. It is desirable that the machine itself should not be breakable on the material that can be expected to be available to the enemy. The Enigma, as used in 1939, fulfilled this condition.

How breaks were secured

If a cipher that is meant to be invulnerable to cryptographic attack is broken, this must be due to a mistake or series of mistakes on the part of one of three classes of people:

(1) The cipher may be broken through an error made by those people who originally invented the system, i.e. there has been an unnoticed fatal flaw in a system regarded as theoretically secure.

(2) The cipher may be broken through an error made by the people who made up the keys, e.g. by a non-random construction of keys. The most flagrant instance of error in Enigma was the key repeats in 1942. This type of error could scarcely give an initial break, but once discovered, it helped to give a whole series of subsequent breaks.

(3) The cipher, even if secure in the above respects, might still be broken by errors on the part of the cipher clerks. An "error" in this case meant any avoidable action by the clerk which permitted the break. In the case of the Enigma, the most important such error was the providing of a crib or cilli. Other possibilities were the provision of ringstellung tips or depths. To exploit such errors, constant decode evidence was necessary.

How breaks could have been be prevented

The general methods of preventing breaks, i.e. achieving full cipher security, were obvious from the foregoing analysis. All the above classes of mistakes must be avoided, and this gave three conditions for the security of a cipher:

(1) The cipher must be theoretically secure, i.e. unbreakable if no errors are made in the construction of keys and encoding of messages.

(2) The construction of keys must be wholly random, i.e. there must be no rules of keys or key repeats (other than such repeats as can occur by chance).

(3) The effect of possible errors by the cipher clerks must be obviated.

Of these conditions, the first two are the easiest to achieve. The Enigma machine, provided it was used with an adequate indicating system, fulfilled the first criterion. But the proviso is important: the first two indicating systems employed by the Germans were quite inadequate. In both cases the Bombe provided an easy theoretical solution on a small amount of traffic, apart from the other methods that were used. It was not till May 1940 that the Germans, by introducing an adequate indicating system, made the Enigma theoretically unbreakable.

The second proposition is largely independent of the exact cipher system employed. The Germans could have easily kept this condition, but they lamentably failed to do so, particularly on the Air keys.

But in practice the third condition is the hardest to keep, and the main reason why theoretical security of the Enigma in May 1940 did not give practical security, is that the Germans failed so badly to control their cipher clerks.

The two roads

How could the effect of possible errors by cipher clerks be obviated? There were, broadly speaking, two methods, but an essential preliminary to using either method effectively is for those responsible for inventing the system to ask themselves what errors the cipher clerks could make, i.e. what they could do which would assist the enemy cryptographers to break the theoretically secure cipher (assuming that the first condition is satisfied). When, by an effort of imagination, this question had been answered, there remained the choice of two roads: either to make the committing of these mistakes difficult or preferably impossible, or to make the machine so much more complicated that the mistakes of cipher clerks would not now be sufficient to break the cipher. An illustration from Enigma history will make this clearer:

To break the Enigma after May 1940 it was necessary to obtain a crib in the widest sense of the term. This was done through errors on the part of cipher clerks and BP broke on cillies, cribs in the narrower sense and re-encodements. To stop this breaking, the Germans had two policies – either to prevent their cipher clerks providing the enemy with cillies, cribs or re-encodements or to complicate the machine so that it should become unbreakable on the material provided. In fact, they adopted both courses, the first by various anti-crib and anti-cilli devices (re-encodements were a blind spot throughout), and the second by the use of Reflector D which (if used universally on a key) made cillies and cribs of normal length unusable for breaking.

The principle of over-protection

If the question is asked: what is the best method to adopt to neutralise the effect of the encoders' mistakes – the method of prevention or the method of further complication – the answer would be – "try both". Logically it may be answered that this is unnecessary. If one has so complicated the cipher that it cannot be broken on the length of crib that can be expected to be given as a result of encoders' errors, then it is, strictly speaking, a work of supererogation to eliminate cribs.

But in practice it was very difficult to be certain that one had fully allowed for all the mechanical cryptographic aids the enemy might have invented (it did not appear from BP's interrogations of German cryptographers that they had conceived the possibility of the Bombe), and so nothing could be lost and much might have been gained by making assurance doubly sure. Thus, if one had a cipher which – as far as one knew – could not be broken on a crib of less than one thousand letters, it would still be a useful precaution to try and eliminate cribs of 30 or 40.

The German Enigma

The Germans attained theoretical security in their use of the Enigma in May 1940, but on most keys they never attained practical security. The German experience provided for all posterity a classic demonstration of the yawning gulf between these two objectives.

The failure of German efforts

Of the three conditions of cipher security, the Germans achieved the first, never properly realised the importance of the second, and failed – despite great efforts and a wealth of ingenuity – to achieve the third. The particular errors they made in their use (or often misuse) of the security devices they adopted have been pointed out previously, and it is noteworthy how often one type of error occurs. Again and again, the Germans introduced new devices in a piecemeal and half-hearted way: "too little and too late" should be found engraved on the heart of the German cryptographer. Such diverse devices as wahlworts and Reflector D all suffered from this radical fault.

Air and Army security

Certain parts of the Enigma complex were more security conscious than others, and by their relative successes, showed up badly the weaknesses of other sections. In particular, Army keys were more secure than Air and hence were, for most of the war, harder to break. This was due to the following reasons:

1. Army keys in general obeyed much better than Air keys the obvious precaution of keeping traffic down to a minimum by the use of landlines, omission of unnecessary reports and other measures.

2. Army keys avoided many of the Air-type of cribs – especially the longer-lived weather cribs.

3. Compared to Air keys, Army keys were usually constructed in a random manner. Their rules and repeats were much fewer.

4. While the Army did not use some of the Air security devices, such as Enigma Uhr, it made much better use of the devices it did employ, for example the correct use of Reflector D by the Army compared with its misuse by the GAF.

Something should be said on behalf of the GAF. The air was much more continually in progress than the war on land, and the generally wider distribution of GAF units made the Army reliance on landlines impossible. Moreover, weather reports were much more important for the GAF than for the Army, and the larger number of Air keys that had to be made up was certainly one reason for the labour-saving devices of their keymakers. While these considerations cannot be regarded as a valid defence for the GAF against the charge of cipher insecurity, they may justly be pleaded in mitigation of sentence. But perhaps the fairest moral to draw is that the more any Service is continually involved in operations, the more vital is the necessity for constant supervision of cipher usage if security is to be preserved.

The special case of Greenshank

In particular, Greenshank showed how secure the Enigma could be made. If the breaking of the A and B keys on the same day is not recognised as two, only nine days were broken on the double indicating system – nine breaks in five years – and seven of these were re-encodements. So, if the Germans had changed the Time of Origin on re-encodements – one of the security measures they never thought of – Hut 6 might have had only two breaks in five years!

How to achieve security

Two subsidiary points should be mentioned – the value of W/T camouflage measures and the possibility of radical improvements to the Enigma machine. On the first point, W/T camouflage, while not of absolutely primary importance in defeating enemy cryptographers – not, that is, in comparison with cryptographic terrors like a new reflector – they are nonetheless useful in a subsidiary way. Every measure which makes accurate key identification of messages from the outside difficult or impossible should be adopted as a matter of course as a supplement to the measures to be described.

Second, it was certainly possible to introduce very radical improvements to the Enigma machine. In particular, the use of a more irregular motion for the wheels and the abandonment of the reciprocal property of the machine would enhance its security value. The first reform at least was definitely contemplated by the Germans, as was shown by an interesting interrogation of Dr. Fricke, one of their cryptographers – he evidently considered the uniformity of the wheel motion as one of the weaknesses of the Enigma machine. But such extensive changes alter the very type of the machine. An Enigma-type machine is generally held to be:

(1) a machine with a uniform motion consisting of the right-hand wheel turning over constantly and the other wheels moving at regular intervals, and

(2) a machine where the text is encoded by a there-and-back process, i.e. by the enciphering proceeding through the wheels from right to left and back again via a reflector, possibly (but not necessarily) with a stecker substitution at each end. Such a machine is necessarily reciprocal.

The following recommendations made by BP at the end of the war underline clearly where the Germans went wrong.

(1) The security of the machine should be such that even if cribs of normal length are available it should be unbreakable – for this purpose the Enigma of 1939 is inadequate. The Enigma, plus a pluggable reflector, is a good answer, provided the reflector plugging is an integral part of the key and no fixed reflector is still used. Pluggable wheels might be an even better solution in theory, though possibly too complicated for actual use. Any such plugging should be changed daily.

(2) As a safeguard against underestimation of the enemy's mechanical ingenuity, stringent anti-crib measures should be enforced. These should include:

> (a) Prevention of cillies, preferably by an indicating system which makes this form of carelessness impossible;
>
> (b) Prevention of cribs by a definite attempt to eliminate as far as possible all routine messages (particularly nil returns) and by use of the "cut" in all messages (see wahlworts);
>
> (c) Prevention of the discovery and use of re-encodements by their elimination as far as possible through a carefully planned system of key distribution, and the systematic camouflage of such as must remain by changing the Time of Origin, altering the form etc.;

3. All keys must be constructed in a random manner.

The Necessity of Supervision

There remained the absolute necessity of a strict system of supervision over keymakers and cipher clerks alike, if the second and third recommendations were to be carried out. It was here that the Germans failed so badly. They had a system of supervision, certainly, and from time to time an exceptionally zealous Security Officer issued an anti-crib regulation or rapped a negligent operator over the knuckles. But it is clear from the German failure on the subject of cribs, that their supervisory system was not thorough enough or sufficiently co-ordinated.

One distinct weakness was that their cryptographers were kept too much in the dark. They were never allowed to inspect genuine traffic or keys, according to Dr. Fricke – consequently they could not check whether the second and third recommendations were being obeyed, and they often were not. It may be shrewdly suspected that the German cryptographers would have been horrified at their cipher clerks' neglect of security and their frequent misuse of the Enigma, but as they were not permitted to inspect genuine traffic, they could not discover the mistakes actually made.

Hence, no doubt, their frequent barking up a wrong tree. There was the German obsession on "depth" (the incidence of two or more messages, or portions of messages, on the same key at the same machine setting), which occurred so seldom that it was not an important factor in breaking. Also, many of the mistakes for which BP criticised the German cryptographers were probably due not so much to their errors, but to the disregard by the German authorities of the advice of their experts.

The general moral seems to be that it is a mistake on fancied grounds of security to keep your own cryptographers in the dark. If they are to be sure that the systems they have invented give not merely theoretical security, but actual security as used, they must be allowed to inspect – occasionally, at least – actual keys and encodes. Theoretical security is not enough, and practical security can only be attained by a constant intelligent supervision of practice.

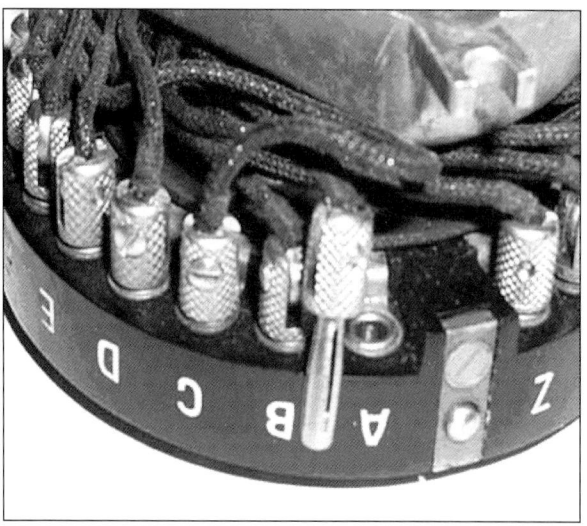

Two views of the pluggable Reflector D.
Photos courtesy of www.w1tp.com

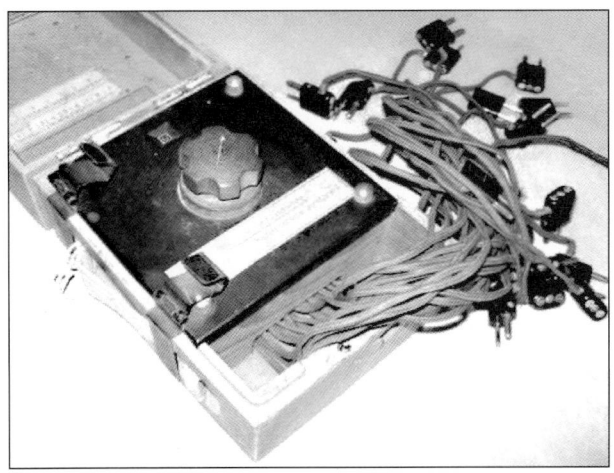

The wires and rotating wooden knob of the Enigma Uhr which changed the function of the plugboard.
Photo: Rijmenants, Dirk. Cipher Machines & Cryptology: http://users.telenet.be/d.rijmenants

The Enigma machine plugboard to which the Enigma Uhr was attached.
Photo: John Jackson